Joseph H. Bolsterli

The Cow-Boys

An original Comedy Drama in five Acts

Joseph H. Bolsterli

The Cow-Boys
An original Comedy Drama in five Acts

ISBN/EAN: 9783337182175

Printed in Europe, USA, Canada, Australia, Japan

Cover: Foto ©ninafisch / pixelio.de

More available books at **www.hansebooks.com**

THE COW-BOYS.

CAST OF CHARACTERS.

Sam Eggbeater, *Owner of Saloon*,.............................

Daniel Mead, *Owner of Ranch*,................................

Jim Burns, *Forman of Ranch*,........ ...   .

Broncho Ned, *Cow-boy*.......................................

Wild Pete,   "   ....

Pat Edward,   "   ....

Billy Cook,   "   ....

Mexican Frank   "   ....

Jack Sutton, *Old Time Cowboy*,...............................

Sleepy Ike, *Driver of Grub Wagon*,..........................

Adolph Cleveland, Jr., *Darkey who works on Ranch*,............

Geo. P. Endy ⎫

H. W. Wilson ⎪

Sam Button ⎬ Cow-Boy Whistling Quartet.

John C. Lewis ⎭

Dorothy Mead, *Daughter of Daniel Mead*,.....................

Bertha Young,...

Edith Young, *Chas. Young's Oldest Daughter*,.........

Mrs. Wallace, *Wife of Ed. Wallace*,.......... ....

Mable Wallace, *Daughter of Ed. Wallace*,.....................

Minnie West ⎫

Dora Mitchell ⎪

Emma Dean ⎬ Cow-Girl Singing Quartet.

Phebe Schenck ⎭

INDIANS.

Shooting Arrow,...
Man Afraid,..
Running Snake,..
Makenoise,..

HORSES.

Brick Top....................................Daniel Mead.
Buck Shot....................................Jim Burns.
Light Foot...................................Broncho Ned.
Badger.......................................Wild Pete.
Barney.......................................Pat Edward.
Star Light...................................Billy Cook.
John the Baptist.............................Jack Sutton·
Comanche.....................................Dorothy Mead.
Prince.......................................Bertha Young.
Ginger.......................................Edith Young.
Badger.......................................Mrs. Wallace.
Pansy..Mabel Wallace.
Slippery Elm, *bucking horse*,...............Jack Sutton.
Gibraltar, *pack horse*......................Sleepy Ike.

STEER.

Commodore....................................Jack Sutton.

DOG.

Bounce,...................owned by Sam Eggbeater.

Violinist, etc., by the Company.

TIME OF REPRESENTATION—ABOUT TWO HOURS AND A HALF.
TIME, the present. LOCALITY.

NOTE.—Indians, in Act IV, can be doubled and played by Girls. Whistling Quartet, in Act IV, can be doubled by Cowboys. Sleepy Ike, in Act IV, can be doubled and played by Sam E. Horses, in Act II and Act V, can be doubled to suit. Singing Quartet, in Act 11, can be doubled by Cow-girls.

SYNOPSIS OF INCIDENTS.

Act I. Scene, Bar-room—Elk Horn Saloon. The Fashion—
Jack Sutton misunderstanding. Introduction. Game of
Seven up. Singing and music. Horse deal. Off for the
ranch. The return. Sutton on the war path. The waltz.
The jump. A bet. Pick up. Excitement. Pool on horse
back —Jack's winnin shot, "here goes for ther king pin." O
ther out-fit. Curtain.

Act II. Scene, The ranch. Adolph in trouble. Burns returns from town, The word. Jack at the dance. Mead ar-
rives at the ranch. Burns gives the orders.

Scene 2. "Good lord how dem folks do eat." Calls Adolph.
All young chickens need ter be kivered well this time o year.
Breakfast. The start.

Scene 3. "I just save dem fo de misses," dey cant do nuffin
less dey axe my vice. "Oh where are you." Bertha and
Edith. Did'nt sprect it am so late. Adolph enjoyment. Good
morning girls. Cow-girl singing quartet on horse back.

Act III Scene, On the plains.—"I wonder where Burns
is." What ails our old ark. Lost ther trail. After a fore-
wheel. Bet a tin horn he'll rowl that kayuse every jump.
—"Here is yer gol-dang wing." Finding the bottle. Drink-
ing.—"Thunder man did you drink that."—I'll see you ride a
bucker before sun-down. You can all ride when you haveto.
—What drove that in your thinker—I want to see Pat make
his ride. Here comes me old friend Jack Sutton. "Help me
saddle him."—Jack rides bucking horse. Curtain.

Act IV. Scene, In Camp. Injun wedden over on Onion
Creek. Its no fun cooking flaps for a hungry cow outfit.
Asleep under grub wagon. What did he train him to do, "he's
going to take him to the fairs." Jumping rope. Pete you
and Ned ride the basin. Who will cook for this layout. Jack
lost his rope. "Hold on I'll turn ther batter.

Scene 2. Arsh darn dese yar skets. Must be gettin married
twice. Iidians going up the pass. Cow-boy whistling quartet. Curtain.

Act V. Scene, Prairie, "Oh Mr. Burns we want some fun." Who ever saw a Virgin reel on a horse's back.—Hold on, you spitfiire—"I knew he would do it." I'll rout-out ther whole cow-camp. "Ladies Mr. Sutton." Charles Young's little gal. Stray critter out ther bunch.—This seems like old times again.—Virginia reel on horse back. Curtain.

COSTUMES ETC.

SAM EGGBEATER.—Act. I. Boots, dark trowsers, light shirt large black neck-tie, white hat, bandana to suit taste. Act IV. Boots, blue overalls and shirt, red and white bandana handkerchief for neck.

DANIEL MEAD.—Act II. Boots, Corduroy suit, gray mixed shirt, black neck tie, white handkerchief, soft black hat, bridle with round cheek pieces, buckle on top, round brow piece with rosettes, oval nose piece, reins 6 feet long to buckle in half breed bit, quirt, spurs, stock saddle, slicker, and saddle blanket.

JIM BURNS,— Act, I, II, III, IV, and V. High heel boots, dark trowsers, light blue shirt, dark red handkerchief, gauntlets, white sombrers, dark red sash, full stamped red leather bridle, silver trimmings, conchas, flat leather reins, full stamped neck and breast strap with conchas, large shield in front, half ring silver inlaid bit, quirt, raw-hide rope, 40 feet, 4 plat, silver inlaid spurs, stamped straps, silver conchas, 44 colts, full stamped holster and belt, full stamped stock saddle with stamped black angora saddle bags and coronas, slicker, blanket, full stamped black angora chaparejos.

BRONCHO NED.—Act. I, II. III, IV, and V. High heel boots. gray trowsers, dark blue shirt, bright red handkerchief, gauntlets, white sombrero, bright red sash, full plat bridle and reins style A, silver inlaid spade bid, quirt, raw-hide rope, 40 feet 4 plat, bull whip 10 feet, silver inlaid spurs, straps and conchas, 44 colts, holster and belt, stock saddle with 24 taps, saddle blanket, slicker, blanket, white angora chaparejos.

WILD PETE.—Acts. I, II, III and IV. Moccasins, Calvary trowsers, buckskin shirt, white handkerchief, gauntlets, white sombrero, stamped leather belt with large buckle, full plat bridle, neck strap, standing martingales, round reins, with plat buttons style B, silver inlaid ring bit, quirt, 40 feet linen rope, silver inlaid spurs, straps and conchas, 44 colts, holster and belt, stock saddle, saddle blanket, slicker, blanket, yellow angora chaparejos.

PAT EDWARD.—Acts. I, II, III, IV, and V. High heel boots, dark trowsers, light gray shirt, dark handkerchief, gauntlets, white sombrero, bright green sash, fiat silver mounted bridle, minus throat strap, flat reins, half breed silver inlaid bit. quirt, 40 feet manilia rope, silver inlaid spurs, straps and conchas, 44 colts, holster and belt, stock saddle, saddle blanket, slicker, blanket, white angora chaparejos.

MEXICAN FRANK —Acts. I, II, IV and V. Fine Mexican boots, green Mexican velvet trowsers, pink silk Mexican shirt, dark red Mexican coat, silk yellow sash, Mexican sombrero, blue satin neck tie, handkerchief to suit taste, Mexican bridle and reins, silver inlaid ring bit, fiat plat hackamore, hair rope. quirt, 40 feet sea weed rope, big silver inlaid Mexican spurs, straps and conchas, pistol or knife, full stamped Mexican stock saddle with backarajos.

BILLY COOK.—Acts. I, II, III, IV and V. High heel boots, dark corduroy trowsers, light color flannel shirt, blue handkerchief, gauntlets, white sombrero, blue sash, silver mounted split ear bridle, plat reins with quirt, silver inlaid bit 40 feet manilia rope, silver inlaid spurs, straps and conchas, 44 colts, holster and belt, stock saddle, and saddle blanket, slicker, blanket, black angora chaparajos,

JACK SUTTON.—Acts. I, II, III, IV and V. High heel boots, jean trowsers, red flannel shirt, black silk handkerchief, silk sash, gauntlets, white sombrero, full mounted silver bridle, plat reins, full silver inlaid bit, quirt, raw-hide rope, silver spurs, stamped straps and conchas, 44 colts blued with pearl handles, holster and belt, full stamped stock saddle, bright red saddle blanket, black and white backarajos with silver trimmings, navajo blanket, slicker leather chaparejos.

ADOLPH CLEVELVND JR.—Act. II. Big shoes, black tights, white trowsers, red flannel shirt, red and white bandana, straw hat, rope suspender, 30 feet manilia rope.

DORTHY MEAD.—Acts. II and V. Lace shoes, gingham dress, gauntlets, white sombrero, apron, leather belt, full stamped russet leather bridle, hair tassels, flat reins, full stamped neck and breast strap, half breed silver inlaid bit, quirt, silver inlaid spur, strap and concho, full stamped double rig side saddle roll around seat, fancy saddle blanket. Act IV. Mask, hair, moccasins, buckskin leggins, fancy blanket.

BERTHA YOUNG.—Acts. II and V. Riding boots, pink gingham dress, gauntlets with stiff cuffs, black straw hat and velvet belt, round hair bridle and reins, round neck strap and standing martingales, half breed silver inlaid bit, quirt, full stamped double rig side saddle roll around seat, fancy saddle blanket. Act IV. Mask, hair, moccasins, buckskin leggins, bright red blanket.

EDITH YOUNG.—Acts. II and V. Riding boots, dark gingham dress, gauntlets with stiff cuffs, light straw hat, red velvet belt, flat plat bridle, silver trimmings, round reins, neck and flat breast strap, half breed silver inlaid bit, quirt, full stamped double rig side saddle, roll around seat, fancy saddle blanket. Act IV. Mask, hair, moccasins, buckskin leggins, black and yellow blanket.

MRS. WALLACE.—Act II. Lace shoes, gingham dress, big sun bonnet, white apron, and gloves. Act V. Full plat round bridle, neck and breast strap, reins with buttons, silver inlaid ring bit, quirt, full stamped double rig side saddle, roll around seat, plain saddle blanket-

MABEL WALLACE.—Act II and V. Lace shoes, checked gingham dress, gauntlets, white sombrero and leather belt, 4 strands 8 plat bridle, round reins, silver rosettes, and conchas on side, silver inlaid spade bit, quirt, spur, strap and concho stamped double rig side saddle, roll around seat, fancy saddle blanket. Act IV. Mask, hair, moccasins, buckskin leggins, red and white blanket.

PROPERTY PLOT.

Act 1.

Newspaper. 1 doz. bottles corks and glasses. Dice and box. 1 six shooter. 1 Winchester 44 cal. 1 towel. 1 box matches. 3 papers and 3 bags smoking tobacco. 2 plugs chewing tobacco. 1 pipe. Pail water. Pitcher of water. Cigarette box. Box cigars and cork-screw for for Sam. 2 five dollar bills, banjo and horse for Pete. Pool cue, balls and horse for Pat. 2 pack of cards, broom and horse for Billy. Mandoline and dog for Mex. F. Gold and silver coins, long gray hair, whiskers, pool cue and horse for Jack.

Act II.

Pencil and book for Daniel. Same for Jim. Plug of tobacco, pipe, matches and pocket knife for Billy. Pack saddle and buckskin strings for Ned. Plug tobacco for Jack. Biscuits, cups, frying pan, coffee and blanket for Cow-boys. Pail of water, tin dipper, coffee pot, tea kettle, wash basin, looking glass, towel, comb, brush, axe and wood for Dorothy. Cups for Bertha and Edith. Basket hoe and banjo for Adolph. Broom for Mrs. Wallace. Horses for Mead, Burns, Ned. Billy, Jack, Adolph, Dorthy, Bertha, Edith, and Mabel.

Act III.

Fore-wheel, dark oval bottle for Jack. Bucking horse for Pat. Horses for Burns, Pete, Pat, Billy and Jack.

Act IV.

Pack saddle, wood, matches, flower, bacon, coffee and pot for Ike. Frying pan, jump rope and steer for Jack. Indian costumes for Dorothy, Bertha, Edith and Mable. Horses for Burns, Pete, Pat, Ned, Billy, Mex. F. and Jack.

Act V.

Horses for Burns, Pat, Billy, Mex. F., Jack, Dorothy Bertha, Edith, Mrs. Wallace and Mabel.

SCENE PLOT.

Act I.

SCENE.—Log soloon. Set bar with chair   Pool balls and cue rack   Card table. chair and keg   Pool table   Box   Antlers, fire-arms, bottles. etc. to suit.

Act II.

SCENE.—Landscape   Set log cabin   with door, step, bench, pail and dipper, window open and hung with lace curtain wild, fiowers in box on window sill. Corral with snubing, post visible   wood pile and axe   spring

SCENE 2.—Horses in corral   Folks all asleep
SCENE 3.—Log cabin with door, step, bench, etc. Seme as Scene 1, in Act II.

Act III.

SCENE. Landscape   Range of distant mountains pale blue. A vast rolling prairie copperish in color. Glimpse of cotton-wood, pecan and oak in the bottoms along hidden streams. Fore-ground struded with bunch grass of promade green, buffallo grass and misquite. Cattle grazing as far as can be seen.

Act IV.

SCENE. IV. Landscape. Mountains prairie. Stream of water, cattle etc., in the distant. Scene 2. Incline pass from   fo   Cow-camp

Act V.

SCENE. V. Landscape. Wallace ranch in the distant, trail leading to cabin door. Grub wagon. Rounding up. Cutting out etc. To the right.

STAGE DIRECTIONS.

The player is supposed to face the audience. R., means right: L., left; C,. centre; R. C., right of centre; L. C., left of centre; D. R. C. in F., door right of centre in flat or back scene; D. C., door centre; 1. E. first entran ; 2 E., second entrance; R. U. E., righ* upper entrance; L. U. E., left upper entrance; 1, 2, 3, or 4 G., first, second, third or fourth grooves; UP, toward the back of the stage; DOWN, toward the audience.

R.   R. C.   C.   L. C.   L.

THE COW-BOYS.

Act 1.

Scene.—*Elk-Horn Saloon. Bar-room. Set bar with chair. Pool balls and cue rack   Card table, chairs and keg Pool table   Box   Antlers, fire-arms, bottles and etc., to suit   As curtain rises* SAM EGGBEATER *is discovered seated near bar   with newspaper in hand reading.* MEX. F. *seated on keg rolling cigarette*   PAT E. *asleep on box*

Sam E. (*reading the fashion*) It wont do for gentlemen to be railing at crinoline any longer, for they have just adopted a fashion as ridiculous—leg-of mutton sleeves. The ladies used to encase their pretty arms in these balloons some thirty years ago, but the absurdity did not last a great while—and now the men must fall into the paganism of leg-of-mutton sleeves and peg top, cossack trowsers. Well, well—it's no use to philosophize on fashion. To dress up to the fashion is to submit to perpetual self-bulesque. (*lays paper on the bar strectehes arms and gaps.*)

      Enter JACK S.   *on horse back whistling.*

Jack S. (*laughing*) Who told yer my gal wore sleeve of mutton trowsers and leg of trowsers sleeves?

Pat E (*jumping up*) Be-jabers we have ye this time Mr. Jacho.

Jack S. (*looking surprised*) What do yer mean? (*dismounts leaves horse standing*)

Pat E. Oh be gor'ra ye no well enuf.

Jack S. (*scratching his knee*) Cant see what yer mean anymore than a blind si-wash.

Pat E. (*advance laughing and slaps Jack on shoulder*) Ye said once ye had no girl, now ye say ye have.

Mex. F. (*arising*) That's right Jack. (*lighting cigarette advance toward Jack*)

Jack S. (*shaking hands with Mex. F.*)   How-dy Frank How-dy.

Sam E. They caught you this time old boy.

Jack S. (*turns shakes hands with* SAM) Hel'lo Sam.

Sam E. (*holding* JACK *by the hand*) How have you been aint seen you in a dogs age?

Jack S. (*drops hand*) Oh tolerable how be you!

Sam E, Fine as an E. fiddle string.

Pat E. Ye can fiddle away thin.

Sam E. (*setting out glasses and bottle*) What's the tune gents?

Pat E. Ah some good old snake eye!

Mex. F. (*pouring out drink in glass*) Well Jack what's on the road? (*passes bottle to* JACK)

Jac'x S. *(pouring out drink in glass)* Never saw a hoof print on ther trail ! *(passes bottle to* PAT)

Enter WILD PETE.

Wild P. How-dy ! How-dy !

Pat E. *(pouring out drink in glass)* Come here Pete and wet yer whistle. *(passes bottle to* PETE) Sam set out a glass.

Wild P. *(pouring out drink in glass)* You started early. *(passes bottle to* SAM)

Jack S. About sun up !

Pat E. Yes and got cooked before grub time.

Sam E. *(pouring out drink in glass)* Well ! *(holding up glass)* Here is to the morning star. *(they all drink and remain)*

Wild P. *(speaking to* JACK) How is Cook ?

Pat E. *(looking at* JACK) Who's this Cookie ?

Jack S. A square man. a good friend and er slick a hand as ever climbed er Kayuse !

Wild P. *(to* SAM) Fill em up.

Pat E. I'd like to meet him.

Jack S. *(pouring out drink in glass)* I reckon it wont cost er fortune eh Pete. *(passes bottle to* PETE.

Wild P. *(pouring out drink in glass)* Nary a dollar. *(passes bottle to* PAT)

Pat E. *(pouring out drink in glass)* That cheap enuf ? *(passes bottle to* MEX. F.)

Mex F. *(pouring out drink in glass)* Here's some one now! *(sets bottle down)*

Enter. Billly C. on horse back.

Sam E. *(extends hand over bar)* Hel'lo Cookie.

Billy C. *(shaking hands with* SAM) Hel'lo Sam ! Hel'lo boys !

Jack S. Bill Cook jine hands with Pat Edward.

Billy C. With pleasure, *(Dismounts leaves horse standing shakes hands with* PAT) How is Mr. Edward's health this fine day.

Pat E. Sam put out a glass. *(passes bottle to* COOK) Niver better have a drink and cool off.

Sam E. (*Sitting out glass*) What is it?

Billy C. Good old straight road! (*pouring out drink in glass, sets bottle down.*)

Wild P. (*handing bottle to* SAM) Dont be backward.

Sam E. (*pouring out drink in glass*) Yours truly.

Pat E. (*holding up his glass and looking at the contents followed by the boys*) Every man sip the morning dew. (*they all drink and remain at the bar.*)

Sam E. How is things at the ranch? (*washing glasses*)

Billy C. Straight as a string an all tied up!

Mex. F. Bill what has become of Broncho Ned, aint seen him in a cows age.

Wild P. I would like to see Ned my-self, most forgot how he looks.

Jack S. He dont grow any shorter. (*laughter*)

Wild P. I reckon not.

Sam E. (*to* BILL *and* JACK) Boys thers a good corral out-side for your hosses, just take them out and have something on me, its no place for them in here.

Jack S. (*leading both horses out   *) Sartainly Sam, Sartainly anything for piece. (*boys talk and fill glasses*)

Re-enter Jack S.   goes to bar and fills his glass.

Billy C. Jack give us some of that jaw-bone lingo about old red eye. (*pointing at his glass*)

Jack S. (*scratching his cheek and uneasy*) Boys I dont no any such notes and when I got to take a speech by ther horns, I'm allus as oneasy as'er maverick in er branding pen and I think yer all off'n yer k'bases when yer rope me fur jaw-bone music. (*boys al-to-gether*) Come, come pan out.

Jack S. (*raises his glass and takes off his hat*)
    Here is to ther man that made ther sun,
        Ther prairie so green fur ther bronck's ter run.
    Fur good wiskey we'll have but never wealth,
        So here goes hands to ther old long horns health.
(*they all whoop, set their glasses on the bar and look at* JACK)

Mex. F. Where did you larn that piece o music.

Billy C. Oh he's handled that since the fall round up.

Jack S. Look a here Bill dont yer go ter throw'n red pepper in my eyes when I'm down.

Billy C. I was only joken pard, shake. (extends hands)

Jack S. (shaking BILL by the hand) Bill I'll forgive yer I al-lus said as how yer was square up one side and down ther other.

Billy C. Jack I'll play you a game of seven-up to see who treats the house.

Jack S. I'll go yer one if I loose a hoof, git ther cards (SAM gives cards to BILLY who goes to the table followed by JACK. they sit down) Cut for deal. (they cut cards, BILLY wins) String em out. (they start to play)

Sam E. Say Frank you and Pete give us some music to livly things up a bit. (gives MEX. F. madoline, PETE a banjo they do sit on the pool table sing a song and play)

Pat E. Yis its music we want. (remains standing at the bar talking to SAM)

Jack S. (as music stops jumps up exclaiming as BILLY, takes a jack from the bottom of the pack) Bill Cook yer a dog-gone cheat I seen yer take that jack from ther bottom.

Billy C. Take those words back or I'll (reaching down laughing)

Jack S. (angry drawing his gun) Not while I kin comb my hair.

Mex. F. (who is watching them) Hold this! (handing PETE his mandoline, jumps down, runs and takes JACK by the arm) Would you plug your best friend?

Wild P. (jumps down, lays mandoline and banjo on the bar, runs between JACK and BILLY) What ails you?

Jack S. (strugling) A man aint yer friend when he cheats at cards.

Billy C. Jack if I done it I don't no it. (laughing)

Jack S. Yer'll say that sometime and choke with a lead pill. (still strugling)

Pat E. (going over to JACK) Ye old tom kitten, what ails ye Bill, was only in fun, for I winked at him to do it.

Jack S. (strugling) Yer sneaking coyote, yer tarnal Siwash, help him ter cheat me, will yer. (puts up his gun and tries to get away) I ring yer neck.

Sam E. (puts away instruments, goes over, takes JACK by the arm) Let go of him boys! (patting JACK on the back) That was only done for a joke. (takes JACK to the bar, followed by the boys) Have one on me.

Jack S. (shaking his head) Not by a dang site, Bill Cook lost ther game and got ter stand drinks.

Billy C. (laughing) Dont see how I could loose it. when you would'nt play it out.

Pat E. (slaping BILLY with his hat) Stop chafin his timper.

Jack S. I would if yer played square.

Wild P. I move, Bill Cook pay for the drinks.

Mex. F. I second that motion.

Jack S. I'll third it. (bringing the but-end of his gun down on the bar, reeling and hold on to PETE) Cut em out lively. (JACK starts to hop and sing, boys remain at the bar looking on)

Mex. F. (catching JACK by the shoulder as he comes near) I hear you want to sell your hoss, now come right down to hoss flesh, what do you hold him at?

Jack S. (flying in a rage) Who said I want ter sell him? I'll bet one dollar and six bits that's one o Bill Cook's yarns.

Mex. F. No, I heard it over on Dry Creek last night.

Jack S. (angry) I don't wonder it's so dang dry over there, if ther lie like that.

Mex. F. I got a "Jim Dandy" I'll swap you and give ten. (walks slowly toward   )

Jack S. Yer never saw money enough to buy that critter. (starts after MEX. F.) Hold on yer greaser, war's that kayuse.

Mex. F. Out back of the corral.

Jack S. (reeling) Bring him in.

Sam E. This is no place to show horses.

Mex· F. Come pard, go have a squint at him.

Jack S. (follows MEX. F.   ) Some people mighty ticular now er days.

Wild P. I hope Frank will get him started for the ranch.

Pat (surprised) Is that his game.

Billy C. Yes, and I hope it will work better than mine did.

Sam E. (shaking finger at BILLY) Don't do anything like that again.

Biliy C. (laughing) We only wanted a little fun.

Sam E. That's al-right—but you no just how he is.

Re-enter Mex. F.

Mex. F. (wiping brow with handkerchief; Well he is off. (looking around discovers dog lieing in) Come bounce! (dog get's up and goes to FRANK, who takes his paws and dances around bar-room singing)

Wild P. I lowe you had a good time.

Mex. F. (waltzing) I did but he is gone now.

Pat E. If he don't turn back.

Mex. F. Oh no he'll pull his freight straight for the ranch. (stops waltzing, dog goes and lies in)

Pat E. (taping MEX F., on his shoulder) I'll play ye a litttle game of draw.

Wild P. If you don't object, I'll jine you.

Pat E. (shaking his head) No pard, I'm just a beginer and I don't mind chaseing one critter, but I can't keap me eyes on two and run both ways at once. (PAT goes to table followed by MEX. F., sits down, gathers up cards commences to shuffle, MEX. F., takes his seat)

Sam E. Pete, l'll just shoot you a game of crap. (gets out dice and box)

Wild P. I am your "cuckoo,"

Billy C. Stay with him Pete. (goes to box sits down, draws hat over his eyes and takes a nap)

Wild P. (shaking dice) Sev come lev. (shakes dice) Long Liz from Kansas. (shakes dice) Brown hoss wins.

Pat E. (uneasy) Jabers it's hot, lets move by the door, so I can get a we drop of air. (move table chair and keg in front of door sit down and game proceed)

Sam E. Good throw, but I'll beat it. (shaking dice, throws) Five. (shakes dice) Eight. (they all stop playing and look toward the door, BILLY sleeps on, where they hear a whoop and a horse on a dead run.

Pat E.   looks out the door, throws up his hand)   God save
us it's JACK SUTTON.

Re-enter Jack S.   on horse back.

Rides through the door with a whoop, jumps horse over
card table.   Into the bar-room and shoots.   Pete runs catches
Jack's horse by the bridle and holds him.   Sam drops behind
the bar.   Billy jumps up, runs and springs on horse, from behind catches Jack by both arms and pins them fast, they
struggle and fall off horse.   Billy holds on to horse.

Billy C.   Are you a fool. crazy, or got a fit.   (BILLY takes
his gun)

Jack S.   (struggles)   I don't froth at ther mouth and can
lick ary puncher in ther out-fit.   (breakes away from BILLY,
runs around bar-room, followed by BILLY. vaults over his
horse, BILLY runs around to get him on the other side   when
JACK vaults back in the saddle, BILLY catches him by the foot
and holds him fast)

Wild P.   Hold on him Cook !

Jack S.   Let go my hoof, or I'll kick out yer front grinders.

Pat E.   (getting up from card table and going over to JACK)
Come, behave your-self, or do ye want to kill some one and
get strung up.

Jack S.   (angry)   Who said I killed him !   Who says I got
strung up.

Sam E.   (rising up)   No one, but you will if you keep on
this way, come get down.

Jack S.   No I won't !

Billy C.   Jack are you going to git of that hoss.   (pulling
his leg

Jack S.   (holding on to saddle horn)   No, No, are you deef.

Mex.   F.   (getting up from card table and taking hold of
JACK)   If you don't get down we'll take you off and hog-tie
you till you are sober.

Jack S.   Who said I was sober.

Wild P.   Come, come git off your hoss he is tired enuf
after that run.

Jack S. He did'nt run, he jis flew and jumped badger holes !

Sam E. Say aint I always been a friend to you?

Jack S. Yes, yer have pard, that's gospel.

Sam E. Then do that much for me and get down.

Jack S. Not till I git my gun.

Sam E. Cook give him his gun. (COOK hand's him his gun)

Jack S. (dismounts, goes to the bar, followed by the boy's) I just uncinch a mite. (goes over and vaults on his horse, boy's remain at the bar filling their glasses, taking down his rope, he catches BILLY around the neck, as they start to drink and jerks him down) Yer will take ther jack from ther bottom and cheat yer pard.

Mex. F. (get's the drop on JACK) You just pan-out that rope, or I'll send leadville clear through you, what do you mean. (takes rope off BILLY's neck with left-hand, covers JACK with right, re-placing his gun)

Jack S. Only a little joke.

Billy C. (rising and rubbing his neck) I don't call that a joke.

Jack S. (wheeling his horse around, coils up his rope and hangs it on the saddle) That's what a said when yer played one on me.

Billy C. Now we are square.

Jack S. Square as a four-bit piece. (showing half dollar to the audience, behind BILLY's back.

Mex. F. (walking over to bar) Come drink up. (JACK pours out a drink in his glass, they all drink and set glasses down on the bar)

Wild P. Jack, they tell me Old John the Baptist is quite a jumper.

Jack S. (smaking his lips) Never was beat.

Pat E. Jump him Pete to see who treats,

Wild P. I'll go him one if I loose !

Jack S. Bring in yer hoss. (PETE goes out   )

Sam E. I would like to know what this is, a hoss corral, or a bar-room ?

Jack S. It's anything we turn in inter; and, some of yer

will get nailed to ther floor. (tapping his gun) If yer don't close your gate.

Re-enter Wild P.   leading horse.

Wild P. Whoa badger ! (patting his horse who stands)

Pat E. Now what the divil are ye's going over one a nuther ?

Billy C. I'll put up something that will make them jump. (takes box and keg to   lays broom across)

Sam E. That's a good jump. (turning to JACK) You can't hop it !

Jack S. Gol-dang my pictur if he clars that I'll ride Old John over it backward. (get's his horse who is standing   ,

Mex. F. You talk like a pap-poose when you say you can ride over that backward.

Billy C. Stay with him pard.

Wild P. (leads his horse to   ) Stand back ? mounts and makes the jump, points to JACK) Come on !

Jack S. (vaults in the saddle, turns, faceing his horses tail) I aint so spry er I was once, but I low no long lean half breed call me when er got a full house. (starts for the jump, clears it, swings his hat, all whoop)

Wild P. Well done hand : I'll treat !

Pat E. I herd he (pointing to JACK) used to pick up a glass of wiskey from the floor backwards between two chairs.

Billy C. Yes, I seed him do it over on Wild Hoss Creek,

Wild P. (dismounts) I'll bet a five it can't be done.

Jack S. I'll kiver it with ar eagle. (throws gold piece on the floor, also his hat and is all excited)

Mex, F. (picking up the coin) I'll hold the stakes. hold-out his hand to PETE who drops in a $5 bill and leads his horse   ,

Pat E. I'll assist. (walking over to MEX. F. If ye nade a rope.

Sam E. Jack ! That must be done out doors, a bar-room is no place for a circus.

Jack S. I never picked up any wiskey out er doors yit and I aint going prospecting now.

Sam E. Well there is no room for it in here; and where would we stand?

Re-enter Wild Pete, door

Pat E. Stand be dang-ed! Sit on the bar and hold the good stuff down, or, he may make a mistake and pick up the whole shooting match.

Mex. F. Come, never mind him and get ready.

Jack S. Bill Cook, yer place ther chairs, and no dang cheating.

Billy C. (placing chairs at) Get out your corn juice!

Same E. (filling glass and giving it to BILLY) There you are.

Billy C. Now mind you don't spill it. (sets the glass down on the floor between the two chairs, get up on the bar followed by PETE, PAT, MEX. F., Pat jumps down again, goes to the glass, drinks half) Ha! What are you doing?

Pat E. Oh, I just took a we sup to see if it was whiskey.

Sam E. Do you think I would keep anything but good whiskey?

Pat E. Oh no, but a calf in the corral is worth two out-side. (gets up on bar again smacking his lips)

Mex, F. (looking at PAT) Now are you satisfied?

Pat E. (laughing) Yes, when I git the other half.

Billy C. Look out, he's ready.

Jack S. (patting his horse) Whoa John? take er easy (lets his horse go, who jumps while JACK picks up glass from the floor) They all whoop. (JACK rides back to dis-mounts, pats his horse) Yer a "Jim Dandy!"

Pat E. (whoops, throws up his hat, twirls gun and starts to jig, music, JACK pats time, PAT stops jiging, picks up his hat, fans himself, goes and replaces chairs)

Mex. F. (slaps JACK on the the back) Well done pard. (hands him the money)

Jack S. (counting) Well that's good interest!

Wild P. (going to JACK) How do you do that?

Pat. E. (feeling lively) How did ye do that now? Aint that a nice question to be asking, How did ye do it, did'nt ye see.

Wild P.   Well yes, but I—

Pat E.   There was no well's there, it was a glass of old red eye, and ye'll niver see yer $5 dollars again.

Wild P.   Oh, I don't care for that.

Pat E.   Nor I nathur, win I can't git it back.

Sam E.   Why don't you try him, Pat?

Pat E.   I'm no rider.

Mex. F.   Try him a game of pool.

Billy C.   (who is taking with JACK)   Say pard, did you hear that?

Jack S.   (surprised)   Hear what?

Billy C.   (pointing)   Pat says he'll go you a game of pool.

Jack S.   I'll go him if I loose a hoof!

Mex. F.   You'll keep on looseing your hoofs till you'll walk on your shin bone.

Jack S.   I never lost ary er one yet.   (putting out his foot and starting for the cue rack   gets one down, returns where the rest are standing, banging it on the floor)

Pat E.   Oh be-gor-ra, I mane on hoss back.

Wild P.   Now you got him!

Jack S.   (who is getting quite tipsy, staggers back to cue rack   puts away cue, takes off his hat, scratches his head and goes straight for the bar)   That's al-lurs my luck.

Pat E.   Are ye going to shoot?

Jack S.   (counting his money)   I'll roll yer a game, git yer critter.   (PAT goes out door   for his horse.

Billy C.   Now Jack, you watch the cut.

Jack S.   I'll head him.

Mex. F.   Come hands give them lots of rope to play on. (they all step back)

Wild P.   I'll bet you are hoodooed.

Sam E.   Snub him, Jack.

Jack S.   Do yer hands think I'm er silver bank?

Re-enter Pat   leading his horse.

Pat E.   I wish ye was for awhile.

Jack S.   (mounts his horse and rides to cue rack selects cue, holds it up, looks at it with one eye)   I reckon as how I mout roll with this un.

Sam E.   Cook, you place them.   (hand Cook the pool balls who places them on the pool table and steps back)

Pat E.   (mounting his horse rides to cue rack   selects cue, rides to pool table and chalks his cue)   That's a fine stick.

Sam E.   (laughing)   All O. K !   Cook, you attend game.

Jack S.   (reeling in his saddle)   Scatter ther bunch.

Pat E.   Here goes to the widdy   (shoots, scattering balls all over table, one drops in pocket)   Ho-ho, me buck-o, I have ye ! (shoots again, ball drops)   Ha-ha, anuthur !   Mon down, (shoots again, missed)   Ah bad luck to ye.

Billy C.   (placing balls in rack   )   Now, Jack Sutton, lets us see you shoot. and don't tear the blanket.

Jack S.   (preparing to shoot)   That yaller pinto for ther small chute.   (shoots ball, drops in pocket)   I knowed I could wing yer.   That brown hoss with ther knocked hip fur ther side corral.   (shoots again, ball drops   I reckon ther comin to fast. can't tie em down: that sneaking   (pointing with cue) coyote fur ther corner hole.   (shoots and missed)   Never could kill er tarnal coyote !   (steps horse back and goes to sleep)

Pat E.   (looking at JACK)   Are ye tired?   (shoots, ball drops)   Ho-ho me girl; Dinnis O'Brien   (pointing his cne) fur the corner,   (shoots ball drops)   I'll wake him whin the game ends.   O'Rafferty for the side.   (shoots ball and missed)

Mex. F.   (goes over to JACK, taps him on the head Stamped !   (JACK awakes quick, looks around in surprise) Come, finish the game.

Jack S.   (rubbing his eyes)   That sleeping beauty   (point) ting his cue)   Fur ther side door,   (shoots ball, drops(Nuther gone ter jine Old Kit; Old Big Toe fur ther corner pen,   (shoots ball, drops)   Mite er known I could rope him.   Calamity Jane fur ther   (pointing his cue)   off side;   (shoots, ball drops) Wiskey Peat fur ther nigh corner;   (shoots, ball drops)   Run_ ning Elk fur the centre tepee;   (shoots ball and missed) Never did have ary luck with er Injun.

Pat E.   His royal highness for the side;   (shoot, ball drops) That hathan China for this corner.   Pointing cue, shoots and missed.   BILLY goes to PAT and whispers in his ear, they smile and point at JACK)

Jack S. Ther Arkansaw traveler fur ther back door; (pointing his cue) nuther passed in his checks. Old Misquite Ike fur the long (pointing his cue) end, O ther branding chute; runs just like it had ther cork out. That small (pointing his cue) gopher fur ther end hole: (shoots ball and missed) I al-lurs said I never could see ther holes in the dark.

Pat E. Saint Patrick for the end; (shoots, ball drops) Here's where I win. Gineral O'Flaretty fur (pointing his cue) Tammany Hall; (shoots ball and missed) Oh the divil take ye. (steps back smiling as BILLY takes ball and goes over to ball rack takes one from JACK'S row and places it with PAT'S, they laugh but JACK who rides around table scratching his head, then rides to ball rack and counts balls while BILLY places the balls for a hard shot.

Billy C. One more, pard, and the game is yours.

Jack S. (stops counting, rides once around the pool table) Here goes fur ther king pin, O ther out-fit! (horse raises and places his fore feet on the pool table, JACK shoots under his horse's neck, makes the shot and wins the game They all whoop)

QUICK DROP.

Act II.

Scene.—Daniel Mead's ranch. Billy C. is seated on bench cleaning six shooter. Jack S. is seated on wiping bridle and saddle as curtain rises.

Enter Horse

Adolph C. (horse takes ADOLPH across from   to on his stomach holding on to rope) Whoa dar! Whoa dar! Yo old fool yo, wait I git on yo back, I done lamb baste yo, I reck-nize who is yo.

Enter Broncho N.   with saddle.

Billy C. (stops cleaning six shooter, looks up) What's the matter with that nigger?

Broncho N. (drops saddle   takes off his cow-whip) That old brown hoss is giving him a sleigh-ride without license.

Jack S. (stops wiping, looks up) That yaller nigger will keep on er monkeying with ther rope till he gets kicked whar he takes his coffee. (spitting)

Billy C. (lights pipe) I reckon you are right, pard.

Broncho N. (starts to plait popper) Bill. things are about as lively here as mud pies. It's three days since I straddled a broncho, I'm getting knee sprung just packing this old carcass around.

Billy C. (smoking) I reckon you'll get all the busting you want, before long, as the boss has dickered for a bunch of Spanish half-breeds for cow-hosses; and, Pete says "they are all wild and wolly and old as Davy Crockett and take your likeness free o charge, head down." A Jack?

Jack S. (spitting Can't say about that, fur Ned aint no tenderfoot and sticks like a Mexican wood-tick. (they all stop work and listen.)

Billy C. (gets up, knocks tobacco out of pipe) Some one is coming full spin, I'll take a squint and see who it mout be. (goes out)

Broncho N. That Bill Cook is a lively puncher.

Jack S. (bitting plug tobacco) Yes, he's more lively when

er wake than asleep; but, a good squar feeder when he feels
well.

Re-enter Billy C.

Bronbho N.   Who is it Bill? (arising)

Billy C.   It's Jim Burns, the foreman, and he is riding to
beat the wind and that means trail work, darn the work ! I
rather lay at the ranch.

Broncho N. (pops cow whip and whoop's)   Now for the
fun.

Enter Jim Burns   on horse back.

Jim B.   (stops horse   dismounts, goes to NED. shakes
hands.
How do you do old pard, glad to see you with us.

Jack S.   (aside   It mout be some one wuss.

Jim B (dropping NED's hand)   Boys, I saw the boss in
town and the word is go after those critters at once, so get
your outfits ready as we hit the road at sun up to-morro w
and must strike camp on Bushy Creek Saturday night: and
to-day is Thursday.   I'll see about the chuck for I'm as
hungry as a timber wolf, and, I think Buck Shot can spoil
some hay. (unsaddles horse and places saddle   leads
horse out   re-enter   throws bridle on saddle and
enter cabin)

Bronch N.   (whoops and pops cow-whip)   We'll pitch camp
on Wild Hoss Creek to-morrow night, and all gin up for they
are good people, there full of fun, and as lively as a Jack rab-
bit. (coils up cow-whip, ties it on his saddle.)

Billy C.   You are right there, Ned, for me and pard (laughs
was over there to a hop last New Year's Eve, and, talk about
fun, why there was more people there than there is here and
old "tangle foot !" why, a whole mess wagon of it; and, you
aught to have been there too, and seen Jack Sutton swing
that maiden.

Broncho N.   (laugh and slaps his thigh)   What Jack Sutton dance? say, people, I would gin my old pinto, pack kayuse, and, lost an eye tooth, to have been there and seen Jack

swing, for I did'nt think he could turn in a Murphy wagon.

Billy C. (laughs) Well, he spun around, all same, and said it was head fun next day.

Broncho N. (shifting six shooter) Say Jack, how is that?

Jack S. (excited pulls at his boot straps) Well, he (pointing to BILL) axed me ter go ter a dance with him over on Wild Hoss Creek, and it's want my nature ter fuse Bill; so, I went and he did git ther laugh on me, fur I told him I was sartan I could dance; but when they commence ter call off in ther new fandango way, I found I was as unsartan about dancing as a mules heel; and, its as Bill said they danced and he danced and I spun around; but, I had gone to far ter back out. so I gin my left side ter a gal and we hit ther floor, then ther music struck up "Yankee Doodle" and all hands shook ther pins. Well. I could'nt dance ter that tune, could'nt larn ter dang tune when I went ter school, but all ther gal's said I was ther best dancer there. so; I kept on deck, till I busted both spenders, then ther all broke camp.

Bronoho N. (BILL and NED langh but JACK looks angry) Well Jack, Bill did have the cinch on you, so we'll chew of him and he buys drinks when we strike the Creek.

Jack S. (BILL hands plug to NED who bites of a chew and passes it to JACK who bites off a chew and puts it in his pocket) He'll buy more than one drink when I tell on him.

Broncho N. What did he do? Come pan out.

Jack S. Well, arter the dance he said (listening)

Broncho N. Spit her out pard, he told on you.

Jack S, Bill says, "will yer git in harness?"

Enter Daniel Mead   on horse back.

Daniel M. How are you boys?

Billy C, Twice two and one to carry.

Daniel M. (smileing, looking from one to another) How are you Jack?

Jack S. (sober) Poor as skim-milk.

Daniel M. Is Burns around? (dismounts leaves horse standing)

Jack S. Yes, he arove a smart spell ago; he's in ther shack I reckon.

Billy C. Ned wher's is that plug of chewing ?

Broncho N. Jack's got it in his breeches pocket.

Billy C. (extending hand to JACK) I'll just relieve you of that weed.

Jack S. (takes plug out of his pocket, bites off a chew and hands it to BILLY) As you axed me civil, I'll oblige you and loan it.

Enter Mead and Burns from Cabin,

Jim B. Take that hoss and give him something to chew, COOK goes to horse, unsaddles him, places saddle   leads horse out   followed by NED and JACK)

Daniel M. When do you think you will be ready to start and what way will you head ?

Jim B. We'll start to-morrow at sun up, camp at Wild Hoss Creek, to-morrow night; Bushy Creek, Saturday night, and pitch camp until Monday. Take the three notch trail to Weavers Landing, there ford the Misquite, head north west, pass Cliffton Ranch to the right.

Daniel M. Why not head north from Bushy Creek and cut off Weavers Landing?

Jim B. We are apt to mire down Fording Mud Creek, and can make better time by keeping the trail.

Daniel M. (takes out his book and gives instructions to BURNS) Round up and cut out one hundred head of beef steers for William Bros., Chicago; drive to Tums Point, where you will find cars waiting; cut out eighty head of two year olds for Morgan & Co., drive them to Cliffton Creek where the Morgan Out-fit will handle them; then, let the boys bring in that bunch of Mexican hosses and pick out what we need and set the boys to breaking. Keep your eyes open and let me known when you return, as I may be at the Fort. (MEAD goes out   )

Re-enter Ned Billy and JACK.

Jim B. Jack, pick two hosses to the man and have them ready at the first streak of day. (JACK goes out   ) Ned, just look to the pack outfit. (NED goes out   ) Come

Cook, help me with the chuck. (BURNS and BILLY go in cabin)

Re-enter Ned   with pack saddle, places it   Re-enter Burns from cabin with coffee pot and frying pan followed by Billy with blankets and cups, they place them Re-enter Jack   singing Jordan bread)   Got them corraled?

Jack S.   Every critter.

Jim B.   Come hands chuck is ready, let's chew and turn in. (they all enter cabin)

Enter Adolph from Cabin.

Adolph C.   (wiping his brow with bandana)   Good lord how dem folk's do eat!   Sprect der won't be nuffin left for dis poor coon ter chew on.   (walks around with hands in his pocket looking up, goes back of cabin)

Re-enter Burns from Cabin.

Jim B.   Adolph!   Come here you black rascal.

Adolph C.   Yes boss, I's comin.

Jim B.   Git a lope on yourself: (re-enter ADOLPH from back of cabin)   Have grub at four o'clock sharp and no excuse for not having it waiting.   (ADOLPH walks around whistling low)

Re-enter Ned Billy and Jack from Cabin.

Billy C.   I reckon I'll take an extra blanket with me.   (goes to   get blanket)

Broncho N.   (goes to   gets blanket)   We'll all need one before morning.   (goes out followed by BILLY)

Jack S.   All young chickens need ter be kivered well this time o'year.   (bites off a chew replaces plug in his pocket, goes out

Adolph C.   Dog-gone dem folks in such a hurry fo de brekfus, why don't dey eat it night-a-fo; and not keep spectible people up all night waiting on dem.   De good paper done say do unto others just like you want em to git back at you. (kneels)

Now I'se lay me down to sleep,
   Hope cow-puncher fry dat meat;
Put on de coffee, make de bread,
   And let dis nigger sleep in bed.
)arises goes out   )

Scene 2 Horses in corral   folks all asleep, soft music
throughout scene. Time, Night.

Enter Burns from Cabin.

Jim B. (goes to pail, takes a drink, pours remainder in
wash basin, washes his face, dries on towel, takes off hat,
aranges hair with his hand, empty out water from basin,
Music stops) Adolph! Git out that nest, come Sutton!
Cook, don't sleep all day! Broncho Ned! Shake your
blankets. (goes out   )
   Enter Adolph C.   rubbing his eyes, goes   chops
wood for breakfast, goes in cabin, starts fire. Enter Jack S.
          followed by Ned and Billy, they go   get bridles
go out   return   leading horses bridled which they
saddle
   Adolph C. (from inside) Roll in cher boys, de brekfus am
done on de table.

Re-enter Burns

Jim B. Well boys, we'll git on the road in good season.
goes in cabin)
   Jack S. (aside) Al-lus do. throwing BURNS bridle, reins
over the horn of his saddle, followed by NED and BILLY, also
lead rope of pack horse, leaves his horse standing   )
Stand thar yer beauty, (follows NED and BILLY in Cabin)
Music.

Re-enter Burns from Cabin.

Jim B. Adolph, bring out that chuck. (enter ADOLPH
from cabin with his arms full of biscuits. Re-enter NED, JACK
and BILLY from cabin) We just take a bite and not strike
camp at noon as I want to save time. (cow-boys take three

biscuits apiece and place them in their saddle pockets roll up, their slicker. and tie them on saddles, ADOLPH goes around takes biscuit out of saddle pockets and puts them in his shirt front, goes in cabin) Ned, is the pack ready?

Broncho N. I'll have it fixed directly! (ties on coffee pot, frying pan blankets etc.) There you are. (slaping pack horse on his hip)

Jim B. (mounting) Are you all ready.

Billy C. Already. (they mount and ride out   )

Scene 3. Log Cabin with door, bench, step etc.

Enter Adolph C. from Cabin with tin plate.

Adolph C. I just save dem fo de missis (takes biscuits out from front of his shirt and places them on tin plate) She won't no dem when dey gits warmed up fo dis am such poor floor, but I never could drink second-hand coffee, so I'll just make some new and keep it hot for Miss Dorothy. (goes in cabin. Re-enter from cabin singing and doing wing steps, stops dancing looks around) Well, dem folks am done gone, and, de goodness knows, I's aint sorry fo dey can't do nuffin less dey axed my vice. (slips suspender off his shoulder, crawls under bench in front of cabin to take a nap)

Enter Dorothy M. from Cabin.

Dorothy M. (comes out to wash but finds water pail empty) Adolph! Alolph!. Oh where are you?—you can never be found when you are wanted. (goes and fills pail from spring returns, places pail on bench, goes in cabin ADOLPH reaches up gets drink of water and goes to sleep again. Re-enter DOROTHY from cabih, washes, combs and braids hair, empty water from basin on ADOLPH who sneaks out from under bench crawls back of cabin) Oh! I do wish Pa-pa would give up ranching and move in town where I could have some companion of my own sex; but Pa-pa would never be contented there, so I must not complain

Enter Bertha and Edith Young   on horse back. (looking up in surprise) Good morning girls, how do you do Oh! I am so glad to see you, and just in time for breakfast.

Berth Y.   We can not stay as we promised Mabel to be over early and she will be waiting for us.

Dorothy M.   Oh, do have a cup of coffee and something to eat for you must be hungry !

Edith Y.   Well I think I can do justice to some coffee for a morning ride always gives one an appitite.   (BERTHA and EDITH dismount, leave horses standing   go   and kiss DORTHY)

Dorothy M.   Adolph !   Adolph ! .

Adolph C.   (in the distant)   Yes Miss Dorothy, I's comin.

Bertha Y.   Dorothy, Mabel said we should be sure and bring you with us.

Edith Y.   Please do not disapoint us.

Dorothy M.   I don't see how I can, yet it would be cruel to disapoint Mabel.   (enter ADOLPH   with hoe on shoulder and basket in his hand)   Where have you been all morning ?

Adolph C.   (taking off his hat) I's done been down in de tater patch hoeing, just got fro; did'nt sprect it am so late Miss Dorothy. (goes and hangs hoe and basket on cabin, walks out·   ,

Dorothy M.   Adolph !

Adolph C.   (behind   )   Yes, Miss Dorothy.

Dorothy M.   Saddle and bridle Comanche at once.   Come, the coffee is waiting. (enter cabin, BERTHA and EDITH remain standing   )

Edith Y.   How kind in her to think of us.

Bertha Y.   Yes, Dorothy, she is so much like her mother ! Always thinking of others before herself, how she must miss her.

Re-enter Dorothy M. from cabin with cups, coffee and napkins on plate.   Edith takes cup, coffee and napkin goes to bench and is seated.   Dorothy sits on door sill.   Bertha remains standing, leaning against cabin.

Bertha Y.   Oh how delicious !

Edith Y.   And such flavor !

Dorothy M.   Yet, sometimes I prefer good spring water.

Edith Y.   It is very tempting.

          Enter Adolph C.   leading horse.

Adolph C. (taking off his hat) Comanche am done ready,
Miss Dorothy.

Dorothy M. (BERTHA and EDITH place cup and napkin on
plate) I'll not keep you waiting. (enter cabin with cup etc.
Re-enter with hat in hand, they mount and ride out   /

Adolph C. (standing) Well de folks am done gone on a
jollification: so I's gwine to joy myself dis mawnin. (enter
cabin. Re-enter with banjo and chair, goes down
plays banjo and sings. Stops, looks over head) I reckon dis
am a fine day to cotch fish suah. (enter cabin with banjo
and chair)

Enter Mrs. Wallace from Cabin with broom.

Mrs. W. (sweeping) The girls are rather late this morning; (stops sweeping, places hand over eyes) I hope they
have not met with an accident at the ford. (drops hand
trurns quick) Oh my there's that speckled hen out again.
(goes out   )

Enter Bertha, Edith and Dorothy   on horse back.

Enter Mabel W.   on horse back.

Mabel W. Good morning girls, (shaking hands) Oh!
I'm so glad you have come, I had almost given up seeing you
to-day.

Edith Y. We where late starting.

Bertha Y. Better late than never.

Dorothy M. And just in time for dinner !

Mabel W. Which Ma-ma will soon have ready and while
we are waiting let's practice those songs. (Turn horses, ride
down   Horses bow, girls sing, turn horses, ride up
     BERTHA and DOROTHY go out   MABEL and EDITH
go out. Re-enter BERTHA, DOROTHY   MABLE and EDITH
     ride down   Horses, pitch, girls sing, turn
horses, ride up   BERTHA and DOROTHY go out
MABEL and EDITH go out   Re-enter BERTHA and DOROTHY
     MABEL and EDITH   ride down   Horses lie
down, girls sing, horses remain down

QUICK DROP.

Act III.

Scene.—On the plains. Landscape in   Curtain
rises.

Enter Billy C. and Jack S.   on horse back. stop horses.

Jack S.   I wonder whar Burns is and what keeps him so
long.

Billy C.   I don't know unless he stopped at Deer Creek
Ranch to see old man Wallace about a chuck wagon.

Jack S.   What ails our old Ark. (dismounts, sits down)

Billy C.   (dismounts, leans on horse)   Why Sleepy Ike
broke it last night when he ran in that badger hole.

Jack S.   I suppose he's glad on it.

Billy C.   (taking off hat) Who do you mean?

Jack S.   (scratching head) Jim Burns!

Billy C.   Don't see what difference it makes to him.   (re-
placing hat)

Jack S.   Bill Cook you act like an old one horn steer, never
could see a hole when anybody wanted to drive you through
it.

Billy C.   Look here you know as well as I. that we have
got to take a chuck wagon or go without chewing.

Jack S.   I won't go without chewin.

Billy C.   Why.

Jack S.   Play, Jim Burns hand.

Billy C.   What's that.

Jack S.   Go over on Deer Creek and visit some dear little
gal, for I heard say as how they where dead stuck on pun-
chers.

Billy C.   Well she is a very nice girl.

Jack S.   They are all slick till you git in harness with en
and then then commence to run back and pitch and when
wimin git ter pitching, ther is no

Billy C.   Shut up, here comes Burns.

Enter Jim B.   on horse back.

Jack S.   (looking at JIM B.) loose ther trail (spitting)

Jim B.   Oh-no (laugh) What made you think that.

Jack S. Look's like you had (spitting) ter run fur it.

Jim B. Well, a man don't like to run without a good cause, and I am sure I had no cause to run.

Jack S. Look's like yer heap will pan out with er full hand.

Billy C. (laugh) How did you find things at the Creek?

Jim B. All in a flutter; but no wagon to home.

Jack S. (aside) I know'd it. (spitting)

Billy C. Where is it?

Jim B. Down to the Diamond G. Ranch, so I'll have to send one of you boys after a fore-wheel.

Billy C. Send Sutton, he likes a wing.

Jack S. Yer gettin to sassy and need a little chap oil. spitting)

Jim B. Jack, just slip over there while your resting.

Jack S. (gets up, mounts, aside) That's er nice thing ter pack on er cow-hoss, but here goes. (rides out   )

Billy C. (laugh) The longer he lives the better he gits.

Jim B. Yes, but he don't. (dismounts   )

Enter Wild P.   on horse back)

Wild P. Jim, Sleepy Ike wants to know what he will do with that old chariot?

Jim B. We'll soon have him so he can move his freight, I sent Sutton in his be-half.

Billy C. Yes, and he'll ride to beat the breeze, for he started off looking kind o'side ways.

Wild P. I'll bet a tin horn he'll rowl that kayuse every jump.

Billy C. (looking and pointing   ) There he comes full spin.

Jim B. Has Broncho Ned got back?

Wild P. Yes, he's down with Frank Close herding.

Re-enter Jack S.   on horse back with wheel.

Jack S. Here is your gol-dang wing.

Billy C. What are you in for?

Wild P. Well, you behind the bars again. (laugh)

Jack S. (angry) Not for stealing sheep. (lets wheel drop BURNS catches it)

Jim B. Come Pete, pack this wheel and the rest of you waddy's, get a move on! (hands wheel to PETE, mounts his horse, rides out   BILLY mounts rides out   followed by PETE)

Jack S. (pointing after COOK) I choke him fur that (dismounts places bottle   mounts rides out laugh)

Re-enter Billy C.   on horse back.

Billy C. (stops, looks at bottle, dismounts, picks it up. pointing after SUTTON) If he knew this he would'nt sleep on the whole round-up : Here goes for prospecting. (drink, spits and shakes his head) Oh lord, geese and Jack rabbits that's old Sutton, Rheumatis liniment mite a known he never left anything good behind.

Enter Pat E.   on horse back.

Pat E. Oh-ho me fine lad, I caught ye this time, give me the bottle, till I have a we sup.

Billy C. You don't need any of this.

Pat E. Aint I been dying with thirst this past two hours.

Billy C. (hands him bottle) Here pass in your checks.

Pat E. Here's to the jack pot.

Billy C. (winking) Let her flow !

Pat E. (drinks, spits, drops bottle, jumps etc. (Oh ! be the holy pipers ye dirty mean, sneakin sheap thief, ye dirty blackgaurd to give a man such stuff to drink !

Billy C. (doubling up his fist at PAT) Look a here, you green gopher, call me that again and I'll knock all your front grinders out !

Pat E. (dancing around for fight) You will, you will will ye? (makes a mark with his foot) Toe that, thin, and I'll put a new horn on your face.

Billy C. (makes a rush at PAT) You'll never !

Re-enter Wild P.   on horse back.

Wild P. Hold on, Hold on, what's all this row about?

Pat E. (pointing) Pick up that old black bottle and taste it.

Wild P. (laugh) Taste it? What's that got to do with you and Cook?

Pat E. Taste it did ye, say? divil a taste fur me I had one. (Cook langh) Laugh will ye? I'll put a muzzle (jumps for Cook)

Billy C. (jumps for Pat) Hold on! You (they clinch)

Wild P. (dismounts) What ails you two fools? parting them)

Pat E. Whin I come in, says Cook, do you want a drink of good wiskey? 1 do says I; well, here says he, and he give me the bottle. I took a nip and it near burnt out me second tongue.

Billy C. That's a lie, you took the bottle.

Pat E. I did, did I? (jumping around)

Billy C. Yes, you did. (laugh)

Pat E. Thin I did, be-gor-ra! If I thought you give it to me I'd shut off your wind machine.

Wild P. What's in the bottle?

Billy C. Don't know. I was comin up the trail, and saw something glitter in the grass, so I stopped, got off to see what it was, picked it up, when, along comes his royal sir (pointing at Pat) and wanted a drink, so I gave it to him.

Wild P. Did he drink it?

Billy C. He just low ed it was whiskey and run it down.

Wild P. Did'nt, you know what it was.

Billy C. No, he did'nt give me time to find out.

Pat E. (picking up bottle) It aint to late now, and, you can drink to your hearts content. (hands bottle to Cook then to Wild P)

Billy C. I don't want it.

Wild P. Whew, what a smell!

Pat E. And it tastes a divilish sight worse! (Cook laugh)

Wild P. (takes bottle and scents it, laugh) Thunder! Hand, did you drink that? Why, that's old Sutton's liniment, he sent to town for and he'll be as mad as a wounded elk, if he finds out who dumped it.

Billy C. I did'nt turn it out.

Pat E.   Well, don't say I did.

Wild P.   (tossing bottle   )   I'll throw it a way and say nothing about it, he'll think he lost it.

Pat E.   He did, and Bill Cook found it.

Billy C.   Yes, and you swallow'd it.

Pat E.   Bad luck to the likes of ye !

Wild P.   Well, drop it.

Pat E.   That's what he did.

Billy C.   (pointing   )   Keep still, here comes Burns, (they mount)

Re-enter Jim B.   on horse bock.

Jim B.   What's up. going to take a lay off?   (looks around)

Pat E.   The sun !   (laughter)

Jim B.   (looking at PAT)   I'll see that you ride a bucker before sun down.

Pat E.   I'd ride a dozen if me back was well.

Billy C.   No, one at a time will do.

Wild P.   Give him Old Slippery Elm. he'll make him ride.

Billy C.   Yes, and he'll want to take out his license.

Jim B.   Well Pat, you ride Slippery Elm.   (BILLY and PETE whoop)

Pat E.   Oh ! Mr. Burns, me back's to sore.   (holds hand on his back)

Wild P.   He'll take the kink out of it.

Jim B.   You are always troubled with some disease when you got to ride.

Billy C.   Yes if he swallows his head, he'll snap your neck.

Pat E.   You niver axed me whin I'm well to ride.

Jim B.   You are never well.

Pat E.   (aside I'll not ride him anyway)   I'll do me best.

Jim B.   You can all ride when you have to, so get him up here.   (rides out   )

Wild P.   Are you goin to ride him ?

Pat E.   Back luck to his dirty hide, I'll go and rope him up now.   (rides out   )

Billy C.   Burns looks like he was mad.)

Wild P.   (scratching his head)   Well, Pat goes to far.

Billy C. Yes. (takes off hat, spins it around on fore-finger) but, he's kind o'good-natured.

Wild P. You are right, pard, he is sort o'good-natured; but, I tell you, that won't sit that hoss.

Billy C. Well, I don't think he will ride him.

Wild P. Why, what drove that in your thinker?

Billy C. Oh, I know Pat too well : he'll run a game of bluff, an some other buster will ride ther hoss.

Wild P. No; No; talk cow-sense; Pat can't get out of it this time, for I heard Burns say that hoss had got to be rid to-day.

Billy C. I'll bet you six bits he don't ride him.

Wild P. It's a go. (shake hands)

Billy C. Come (mounts). on We had better spin along, or he'll give us a bucker.

Wild P. I want to (mounts) see Pat make his ride.

Billy C. Oh, we'll be back before he rides. (BILLY and PETE ride out   )

Re-enter Pat E.   leading Slippery Elm.

Pat E. (shaking his fist after PETE) Ye want to see him do ye? Well he will not ride this day, (scratching head) but I don't see how to get out of it. (turning in saddle pointing) Ah, here comes me old friend, Jack Sutton, I get him to help me saddle the slippery mon : thin he can ride him.

Re-enter Jack S.   stops

Jack S. Been fishin ?

Pat E. Yis, don't ye think I caught a Jim Hickey ?

Jack S. Oh, considerin. (speaking to horse) Go on.

Pat E. Hold on, Jack; help me bridle this gent, as I hurt me hand taking me dalleys.

Jack S. Whoa ! (stops, dismounts, leaves horse standing   ) I'll lend a hand if yer right smart about it. Goes and puts handkerchief over horse's eyes and helps put on PAT'S saddle) What are yer goin ter ride him fur ?

Pat E. I wus goin to ride him fur Pete, as he hurt his back last night, and axed me if I would'nt git ye ter ride him; but I did'nt like to ask so much of ye, and now how will I get on with me sore hand.

Jack S. Well. I spose it's alright; but, I don't see what they want ter use this tarnal old out-law fur.

Pat E. (holding his hand) Be·dad, I'll have to git ye's ter ride him after all.

Jack S. Well, I'll ride at it, considerin Pete wants him rid. (mounts and rides)

Re-enter Burns and Wild P.

Re-enter Billy C. and Mex. F.

Billy C. (laugh points at PETE) I told you. Come, hand over that six bits. Music.

QUICK DROP.

————

Act IV.

Scene.—In Camp.—Ike is seated on pack saddle   chin resting in his hand and elbows on his knees, singing softly as curtain rises.

Enter Mex. F.   on horse back.

Mex. F. Hel-lo, Ike, what do you know ?

Sleepy I. Nuthin, only I heard tell ther's er Injun weddin over on Onion Creek.

Mex. F. I'd like to be over there an see it.

Sleepy I. Yes, I s'pose so; but there invites don't go to a cow puncher.

Mex, F. Any of the cow-hands showed up. (dismounts)

Sleepy I. No; but they will be here soon, fur I just saw them come over the divide. They ride like a hungry set, and I mount as well start fire.   gets up, stretches arms)

Mex. F. Yes, and have old flap jacks. I most forgot how they taste.

Sleepy I. I wish you had to cook 'em. It's no fun cooking flaps fur a hungry cow-out-fit,

Enter Jim B.   on horse back.

Jim B. Whew snake peters and cheese. (dismounts)

Sleepy I What's up ! Stampede or man drown'd?

Jim B. No; but it was so hot the tail end of the day.

Mex. F. Whar was you?

Jim B. Down in ther lower basin. and it was hot enuf to crack the back of a turtle.

Sleepy I Jimmine geese wax, I did'nt feel him.

Mex. F. Who? (mounts)

Sleepy I. Mr. Hot.

Jim B. Where was you? (smiled and mounts)

Sleepy I. Asleep under the grub wagon.

Jim B. (nods his head) I'll take good care you don't sleep to-night- (rides out   )

Mex. F. Yes; give him double watch. (rides out   )

Enter Pat E.   on horse back.

Pat E. Whoa ! Barney. (stops horse   ) Hel-lo, Ike.

Sleepy I. Hel-lo, yourself.

Pat E. Ike.

Sleepy I. What.

Pat E. (scratching his head) Did ye see ary a mon around here that looks like me-self ?

Sleepy I. (surly) Yes.

Pat E. Name the ginıleman. laugh dismounts)

Sleepy I. Old Commodore.

Pat E. Who's mother is he the father of ?

Sleepy I. (smiles) Jack Sutton's old trained steer.

Pat E. What did he train him to do ? Eat grass ?

Sleepy I. He larned him to jump rope last Winter, and they say there's a fortune in it fur him.

Pat E. Why don't he take it out of him and give up punching cows. (smiles)

Sleepy I. He is goin to take him to the fairs this Fall.

Pat E. Fur what ?

Sleepy I. To jump rope, I told you.

Pat E. To jump rope, did ye say?   Look a'here Ike (catches IKE by the arm) That's enuther one of your whap-pers. Jump rope, is ıt : Now, how in the name of me father can an old clumsy steer jump rope whin he has'nt divil a hand to turn a string ? (laugh and walks around)

Sleepy I. (pointing at PAT) He's thicker nor wagon grease.

Pat E. What's that ye say?

Sleepy I. I said he could.

Pat E. I'll bet he can't; come. now, (puts hand in his pocket   don't be a snake in the grass.

Sleepy I. What'll you bet.

Pat E. A quart of good tequile.

Sleepy I. You loose. (goes to   ) Hel-lo, Jack.

Jack S. S. (in the distant) What do you want?

Sleepy I. Come up the line.

Pat E. (aside) Loose, did he say?   (winking) I can see me comin now with er stick in.

Enter Jack S.   on horse back.

Jack S. (stop horse   ) What's yer hurry ? Goin ter a dance ?

Sleepy I. No such good luck; Pat bet me a quart of good tequile that commodore could'nt jump rope.

Jack S. Did yer take him up?

Sleepy I. I did.

Pat E. (aside) And he lost.

Sleepy I. Will yon make him jump.

Jack S. Yes, fur two pints.

Pat E. Two pints ! Why don't ye take the whole business ?

Sleepy I. I'll give you half.

Jabk S. I'll go you if I loose my scalp.   (rides out after steer)

Pat E. Be-dad, I'll have his scalp this time.

Sleepy I. Did'nt I tell you he could do it.

Re-enter Jack S.   on foot leading steer.

Pat E. Now, let him go and do the jump.

Jack S. (mounts and steer jumps rope) Now, whar's yer juice ?

Pat E. (excited) Hold on, yer a cheat. That's what ye are. Keep that rope still an lets see him jump it. (runs monnts horse, rides out   )

Sleepy I. Here comes Burns. (runs out   )
Jack S. Whoa! (dismounts leals steer out   )

Re-enter Jim B.   on horse back.

Jim B. (looks around) Al] on 'er strike.

Enter Wild P.   on horse back.

Enter Broncho N.   on horse back.

Broncho N. (whistle places hand on stomach) I could eat a cow.

Jim B. Pete you and Ned ride through the basin, I'll go the trail and meet you at the divide. We'll make a circle ride back to camp. By that time grub will be ready. If Ike don't forget to wake up. (rides out   PETE and NED rides out   )

Re-enter Sleepy I.   on foot, goes to   sits down, twirls hat on fore-finger whistling softly.

Re-enter Mex. F.   on horse back.

Mex. F. (stops horse   ) Well, how about something to chew on? (dismounts)

Re-enter Broncho N.   on horse back.

Broncho N. (stops horse   ) That's what I say.

Sleepy I. I would had grub ready an hour ago, but Frank 'lowed as how flaps would taste him about in the middle.

Broncho N. Can't say I'm stuck on 'em, but I'll gamble I can eat as many as ary puncher in ther out-fit.

Mex. F. Who will do all the cooking for this lay-out. (unsaddles and bridles, places them   )

Re-enter Jim B.   on horse back.

Jim B. stops horse   ) Ike or Bill Cook. (unsaddles and bridles, places them   )

Re-enter Billy C.   on horse back.

Billy C. Who said pie? (stops ho.se   dismounts)

Sleepy I. If your grinders are so poor, you can't chew baked beans an want ox tail soup, you can do yer own cooking or chaw leather.

Re-enter Pat E.   on horse back.

Pat E. (stops horse   ) What's the matter with the bill o'fare? (laugh, dismounts)

Jim B. What tickles you?

Pat E. Oh. be-jabers; ye's missed half yer life. (unsaddles and bridles, places them   )

Billy C. (surprised) Tell us how.

Pat E. Well, ye's know that old split-ear. goggled eyed steer we had so much trouble with last night.

Mex. F. What about him.

Pat E. I wuz trying to keep him in the cut, do ye see? Whin up comes Jack Sutton and says I, Jack ! What. says he Do ye see that old brindle gintleman (pointing) says I. I do, what ails him, says he. I can't keep him in the bunch. What'll we do with him? says I. Rope him and sew up his eyes, says he. Will that bring him to his skimmilk, says I Yes says he. Will ye help me, says I. 1 will. says he. Git down your rope, says I· Are ye ready? says he. I am, says I Thin off goes Jack, an away runs his lordship, and I after the both of them. Jack heads him to me. Capsize him, Pat, says he. I will, says I, and threw me string.

Wild P. Did you bump him?

Pat E. Oh, no; me old McCarthy was'n't long enuf. and I cut him to Jack : He lets fly at his nobility. an caught him in the bud, but that old sog-eyed hoss would'nt hold divil a pound, and away wint the steer to the river with his rope, and he in after him across the water, and up the other side they go; and ye's talk about ther rocky road to Dublin. Dang a road is there that has as many turns as they made. So I rides to the bank and hollows, come on. Jack, and let the Gineral go.

Jim B. What did he say?

Pat E. Ye had better axe him yer self, for I'll not tell ye's.

Mex. F. Well, what did he do?

Pat E. I role ter camp and left him sitting on old sog-eye with ther creeping paralysis, watching the old steer go over the hill.

Wild P. Wait till he strikes camp.

Jim B. Ike get that fire goin, so we'll have something to chew on. (IKE goes   lights fire, puts on coffee pot, etc.)

Mex. F. Who's goin to cook ther flaps?

Jim. B. Jack Sutton fur losing his rope.

Re-enter Jack S.   on horse back, rides to   unsaddles and bridles; places them

Wild P, Hod-dy. old man; some one said they saw you go under water, and Ned said you were sure drowned.

Jack S. (angry) Ducks don't drown so easy.

Billy C. (laugh) There was a motion made in camp and seconded that you cook flaps for this lay-out or take a good chapping.

Jack S. (nodding his head) I won't take a chapping, or turn a flap, nary one.

Billy C. Yes you will.

Jim B. If he don't, chap him. (PETE and MEX. F. catch JACK and hoist him on BRONCHO N. back, PAT gets chapaijoed) Give it to him.

Pat E. (chaps in hand goes to JACK) I'll give him an extra one fur running the steer away. (brings chaps across JACK) That one for the Gineral (JACK struggles, and this is fur me-self. (bring chap across JACK, all whoop)

Jack S. Hold on, I turn ther batter.

Pat E. I thought that would bring him. (boys release him)

Jack S. (goes to   pours out batter, cooks flap jack) Here your are. (turns flaps) I hope ther'l blister yer so yer can't set. (prepare for meal, steer goes from   to dragging rope)

Boys at Supper.

Pat E. What are you thinking of?

Wild P. I was just thinking how I would like to knock off an go see a good hoss race, aint seen one since I quit old Mex.

Mex. F. Come go with me this Winter.

Billy C. Where are you goin to hang out?

Mex. F. Mexico City.

Wild P. I'll go you.

Pat E. I'll raise you two better.

Jack S. They'l kill you down thar.

Pat E. What fur?

Jim B. For gittin in trouble like you do here.

Jack S. It aint his fault.

Billy C. They tell me you have fine times down there.

Mex. F. All kind of sports and fandangoes.

Broncho N. Jack, aught to go, he likes dancing ah, pard?

Jack S. Oh, fairly. (JACK replaces cooking untensils, etc.)

Jim B. Come, it's your watch. (IKE mounts, rides out
)

Scene 2.—Incline pass, from   to   camp.

Jack S. Arsh darn dese yar skeets. (slaps hand)

Wild P. Let go your hold. (slaps his neck)

Billy C. Big as a pie (slaps his cheek)

Jack S. Whoa! What ails that critter? (horse uneasy)
Some un powlen er round (takes gun out of holster) I'll
just keep an eye squinted, and ther first thing comes near
camp, out goes ther bottle stopper.

Mex. F. What's up?

Jim B. Something astir.

Billy C. What is it?

Broncho N. Its those injuns going up the pass from ther
hoe down. (Indians go up pass)

Jack S. Confound ther smoked carcas; they must be gettin
married twice.

Wild P. Hand's, things are kind o'lonesome, whistle or
sing a song to lively us up a bit.

Cow-Boy Whistling Quartet.

Jim B. Come, roll in. (all get blankets and lay down)

SLOW DROP.

Act V.

Scene.—Prairie; as curtain rises, Jim B. is discovered stand-ing watching

Enter Edith Y.   on Foot.

Edith Y. Oh, Mr. Burns, we want some fun, and I have come to you to help us out.

Jim B. (turning) Well, I am a poor hand to have fun with.

Edith Y. (smileing) You don't understand me.

Jim B. Don't you think I know what fun is?

Edith Y. No; No; (stamping her foot) We want you to get the boys together.

Jim B. For a round up?

Edith Y. Oh, no. (tossing her head) For a Virginia reel on horse back.

Jim B. Who ever saw a virgin reel on a horse's back?

Edith Y. (angry) Not a virgin on horse back, but get partners for a dance.

Jim B. (doubting it) Never heard tell of it. Don't see how it can be done.

Edith Y. Well, Jack Sutton knows all about it, for papa and he used to dance it when they where young.

Jim B. (laugh) He know's everything, but his A. B. C.

Edith Y. You can't say yours backwards. (starts off)

Jim B. Hold on, you little spit-fire, don't go pitching too high (EDITH stops) don't you know this is our busy time.

Edith Y. We did not think of that, and do not wish to inter-fer with you work.

Jim B. I'll go see what all this tomfoolishness is about, and if he don't explain some one will catch it. (goes out)

Edith Y. (smileing) I knew he would do it. I'll run and tell the girls to get ready. (runs out)

Re-enter Jim B. and Jack S.   on horse back.

Jim B. Say (faceing JACK) what's all this foolishness I hear you have been stuffing those girls about?

Jack S. (looking up) Never did nuthin o'ther sort.

Jim B. Well, what's all this report about reels and gin reels on hosses? (JACK takes out plug of tobacco, bites off a chew and remains silent. (BURNS shakes him) Are you deaf?

Jack S. I don't hear so.

Jim B. Did you ever dance if or see any one who did?

Jack S. (spitting) I reckon as how I danced at it when I was a'four-year-old.

Jim B. Well. get the boys together, and I'll go see the girls. (rides out   )

Jack S. (uneasy) Who in the dickens and green rattle snakes ever told him about is? He's gone sure crazy or been to some o'them wimin fortune tellers: cause a man aint got no sich sense; for old Uncle Adam never had sense enuf ter git er blanket ter kiver himself. Howsom-ever I'll rout out ther whole camp and set em all er fire. (rides out   )

Enter Edith, Bertha and Dorothy   on horse back.

Edith Y. Come, girls, hurry, for the boys will soon be here.

Enter Jim B. and Mabel   on horse back.

Mabel W. Why, girls, how you must have ridden to get here before us.

Dorothy M. (smileing) The surest way here would naturly be the longest.

Re-enter Jack S.   on horse back followed by Ned, Billy and Pat, who advance and shake hands with the girls. JACK remains   )

Jim B. Ladies, Mr. Sutton, at your service. (JACK raises his hat)

Edith Y. (advancing) Why, how do you do? (extend hand) Don't you know me?

Jack S. (shakes hands) Can't say I do. Recollect ther brand? What mout it be?

Edith Y. Papa brands his stock D., half circle.

Jack S. Then you must be Charley Young's little gal. Why I used to hold you when you were a smooth yearlin. (smiling) but you would be a whole arm full now. (raises hat and peeps in her face) Your a slick one but, I'll be hanged, if you are as handsome as you Mam.

Edith Y. I'm Papa's oldest girl.

Jack S. How many has he got?

Edith Y. Only five.

Jack S. (whistles) Well, I could never beat three of a kind. (EDITH goes and joins BILLY C.) Boys, pluck your pumpkins. Boys get their partners) Forward. Stray Critter out ther bunch. (all laugh)

Bertha Y. (aside) What does he mean?

Billy C. (aside) One short in the dance.

Mabel W. I'll go and get Mama to help us out. (rides out)

Jack S. (aside) I'm sure corraled this time, but here goes, or tear up the snubbing post.

Enter Mabel and Mrs Wallace on horse back,

Mrs. Wallace (goes up head shakes hand's with JACK. He removed her bonnet and hangs it on saddle horn) This reminds one of old days gone by, when we where young.

Jack S. Didn't know wimin folks ever got old.

Calls Off.

All forward and back,
First couple down ther line.
First lady.
Right hand.
Left hand.
Both hands.
Royal swing.
All shake yer pins.
First couple balance to place.
All forward, cross over and back.

CURTAIN.